D0847607

SPACE FIRSTS™

VALENTINA TERESHKOVA
The First Woman in Space

Heather Feldman

The Rosen Publishing Group's
PowerKids Press™
New York

For my mom, Cynthia Wane, for always being there, as the greatest mother and the greatest friend. You are my hero.

Published in 2003 by The Rosen Publishing Group, Inc.
29 East 21st Street, New York, NY 10010

First Edition

Editor: Nancy MacDonell Smith
Book Design: Mike Donnellan

Photo Credits: Cover, pp. 11, 16, 20 (right) © Bettmann/CORBIS; pp. 4, 8, 16, 20 (left) courtesy of the private collection of Alla Pavlova; pp. 12, 19 © Hulton-Deutsch Collection/CORBIS; p. 7 © Photri Microstock Inc.; p. 15 © Roger Ressmeyer/CORBIS.

Feldman, Heather.
Valentina Tereshkova : the first woman in space / by Heather Feldman.— 1st ed.
    p. cm. — (Space firsts)
Includes bibliographical references and index.
ISBN 0-8239-6246-6 (library binding)
1. Nikolaeva-Tereshkova, Valentina Vladimirovna, 1937——Juvenile literature. 2. Astronauts—Russia—Biography—Juvenile literature. 3. Astronauts–Soviet Union—Biography—Juvenile literature. 4. Women astronauts—Soviet Union—Biography—Juvenile literature. [1. Nikolaeva-Tereshkova, Valentina Vladimirovna, 1937– 2. Astronauts. 3. Women—Biography.] I. Title.
TL789.85.N48 F45 2003
629.45'0092—dc21

2001006028

Manufactured in the United States of America

Contents

In 1963, Valentina Tereshkova became the first woman in history to travel in space. Tereshkova was born in Maslennikovo, Russia, on March 6, 1937. At that time, Russia was part of a country called the Soviet Union. Her father was a tractor driver. Her mother worked in a factory that made cotton fabric. Tereshkova had a brother and a sister. Her family lived during difficult times and worked very hard. Tereshkova helped with the work around the house, so she was not able to start school until she was almost 10 years old.

When Tereshkova was 18 years old, she joined her mother and sister and started working at the cotton mill. She continued her education by taking classes at night.

As a young woman, Tereshkova never dreamed that she would one day make history as the first woman in space.

The Space Race

During the 1950s, the United States and the Soviet Union began a power struggle known as the space race. It began when the Soviet Union **launched** *Sputnik 1*, the first **satellite**, into space. Both countries were eager to make their space programs the best in the world. They were in a race to be the most powerful and the most advanced country in the world. There were many firsts to achieve. The first man in space, the first mission to reach the Moon, and the first space station were just a few examples. One of those firsts would greatly change the life of Valentina Tereshkova. In 1961, Yuri Gagarin became the first man to journey into space. His adventure inspired Tereshkova. Little did she know that one day she too would make history for the Soviet Union as the first woman in space.

Sputnik 1 was the first satellite. By launching Sputnik, *the Soviet Union took the lead in the space race.*

Tereshkova's New Hobby

In 1959, Tereshkova joined a sports club to learn how to jump from a plane using a **parachute**. Tereshkova became very skilled at parachute jumping. This was a dangerous and daring hobby. On one jump, Tereshkova landed in the Volga River and almost drowned. This didn't **discourage** Tereshkova. She kept on jumping, and, by 1961, Tereshkova had completed more than 125 jumps! After Gagarin's historic flight, Tereshkova became very interested in spaceflight. She wrote a letter to the **Soviet Space Commission** asking if she could train to become a **cosmonaut**. Her letter was put on file along with thousands of others just like it.

Yuri Gagarin was the first man in space. He was a hero to people all over the world, and he inspired Tereshkova's dream to journey to space.

Choosing Tereshkova

In early 1962, the Soviet leader Nikita Khrushchev decided that the Soviet Union was going to score another first over the United States. The Soviet Union was ready to send a woman into space. Khrushchev asked the Soviet Space Commission to review the letters it had received in 1961. Khrushchev was not looking for highly skilled Soviet women scientists or airplane pilots. He wanted an ordinary Soviet worker to be the first woman in space. From thousands of people who had written letters asking to be cosmonauts, Valentina Tereshkova and four other women were chosen for cosmonaut training. On February 16, 1962, Tereshkova learned that she was going to train to be a cosmonaut.

Nikita Khrushchev was the Soviet premier, or leader of the government, from 1958 to 1964. He wanted the Soviet Union to win the space race.

Cosmonaut Training

Tereshkova was told to keep her training a secret from her family and friends. She told them she was training for a women's skydiving team. For the next 18 months, this cotton mill worker trained to become a cosmonaut at the Baikonur Space Center. Tereshkova was put in an **isolation chamber**. She made parachute jumps in a space suit. She learned to work in weightless conditions to prepare for the lack of **gravity** in space. She also received jet pilot training. Tereshkova found space **technology** and rocket science difficult to learn, but she studied and worked very hard. Soon she would be ready for her historic mission.

In her training, Valentina Tereshkova learned how to eat in the weightless setting of space.

The Launch

On June 16, 1963, Valentina Tereshkova boarded the *Vostok 6* rocket that would carry her on her journey. At 12:30 P.M., Junior Lieutenant Tereshkova became the first woman in history to be launched into space. For her space journey, Tereshkova was given the radio name Chaika, which is Russian for "seagull."

As she journeyed into space, Tereshkova spoke these words on her radio: "I see the horizon. A light blue, a beautiful band. This is Earth. How beautiful it is! All goes well." Tereshkova was on her way!

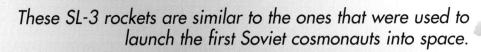

These SL-3 rockets are similar to the ones that were used to launch the first Soviet cosmonauts into space.

Once in space, Tereshkova made 48 **orbits** in *Vostok 6*. This means she circled Earth 48 times! It took her about three days to do this. She traveled 1,200,000 miles (1,931,213 km)! She even came within 3 miles (5 km) of another Soviet cosmonaut in space. This cosmonaut was Valery Bykovsky. He was piloting the *Vostok 5* rocket that had launched two days before *Vostok 6*. While in space together, the two cosmonauts talked to each other through their radios and sent television pictures back to Earth. Tereshkova was seen smiling on television, while her pencil and logbook floated weightlessly around her! Although she experienced a little motion sickness, Tereshkova's successful flight showed that women react as well in space as men do and can handle the **stresses** of space travel as well as men can.

This photo of Tereshkova (third from right) *and other Soviet cosmonauts was taken soon after Tereshkova returned from her historic journey.*

Returning Home

After almost three days in space, it was time for Tereshkova to return home. She needed to fire the **retro-rocket** to get her capsule back to Earth. As her space **capsule** reentered Earth's **atmosphere**, flames surrounded the capsule. Luckily the flames were quickly under control. Tereshkova was **ejected** through the side **hatch** of her rocket, 20,000 feet (6,096 m) above the ground. She parachuted her way down and landed in Kazakhstan, in central Asia.

On June 22, Tereshkova was named a Hero of the Soviet Union, a great honor. She received many awards. Tereshkova traveled the world and made speeches about her incredible trip to space.

When they got back to Earth, Tereshkova and Bykovsky were honored by Premier Khrushchev in a public ceremony in Moscow.

The Space Family

During cosmonaut training, Tereshkova had become friendly with another cosmonaut, Andrian Nikolayev. Nikolayev had orbited Earth 64 times in 1962. On November 3, 1963, Tereshkova and Nikolayev were married in Moscow, Russia. Soviet leader Nikita Khrushchev, along with other top government leaders and space program leaders, attended the wedding.

Tereshkova gave birth to a baby girl, Yelena, on June 8, 1964. Doctors were extra careful in checking Yelena. They were afraid that Yelena's parents' time in space might have affected her health. The baby was perfectly healthy. Yelena was the first child born to a mother and father who had both traveled to space.

Tereshkova, Nikolayev, and their daughter, Yelena, were the first space family! Inset: *Nikolayev was a member of the Soviet armed forces.*

Women in Space

Valentina Tereshkova never traveled to space for a second time. She continued to tour the world and to talk about her experience. She also became very active in the Soviet government. Tereshkova and the other women cosmonauts were never really considered part of the Soviet space program. The women's cosmonaut training program was canceled shortly after Tereshkova's flight. In fact the Soviet Union did not send another woman into space until 19 years after Tereshkova's flight. The second Soviet woman in space was Svetlana Savitskaya, in 1982. On June 18, 1983, Sally Ride became the first American woman to make a voyage to space. It was Tereshkova's brave first flight that paved the way for women of future generations to travel to space. Tereshkova will always be remembered for her historic journey.

Glossary

atmosphere (AT-muh-sfeer) The layer of gases that surrounds an object in space. On Earth, this layer is air.

capsule (KAP-sul) The small, pressurized cabin of a spacecraft.

cosmonaut (KOZ-muh-naut) The Russian word for astronaut.

discourage (dis-KUR-ij) To deprive of courage or confidence, to deter.

ejected (ee-JEKT-ed) To be driven or thrown out from within.

gravity (GRA-vih-tee) The natural force that causes objects to move or tend to move toward the center of Earth.

hatch (HACH) The doorlike opening in a spacecraft.

isolation chamber (eye-suh-LAY-shun CHAYM-bur) A small, enclosed compartment where astronauts are left alone for a period of time during training for spaceflight.

launched (LAWNCHD) Pushed a spacecraft into the air.

orbits (OR-bits) Circular paths traveled by one body around another body in space.

parachute (PAR-uh-shoot) A large device of fabric, similar to an umbrella, that opens in midair and allows a person or an object to descend at a safe rate of speed, as from an airplane.

retro-rocket (REH-troh-rah-kit) An engine that is fired to bring a spacecraft back to Earth.

satellite (SA-til-eyet) A human-made or natural object that orbits another body.

Soviet Space Commission (SOH-vee-et SPAYS kuh-MIH-shun) The part of the Soviet government that controlled the space program.

stresses (STRES-iz) Physical, mental, or emotional tension.

technology (tek-NAH-luh-jee) Industry that deals with electronics and computers.

Index

Web Sites

Due to the changing nature of Internet links, PowerKids Press has developed an online list of Web sites related to the subject of this book. This site is updated regularly. Please use this link to access the list:
www.powerkidslinks.com/sf/tereshk